I0085923

Times and Tides

a memoir: essays of the coast

by
Belva Ann Prycel

*Essays, cover, and illustrations by Belva Ann Prycel

Goose River Press
Waldoboro, Maine

Copyright © 2013 Belva Ann Prycel.

All rights reserved. No part of this book may be reproduced
in any form without written permission from the publisher,
except by a reviewer who may quote brief passages in a review
to be printed in a newspaper or magazine.

Library of Congress Card Number: 2013906153

ISBN: 978-1-59713-140-7

First Printing, 2013

Published by
Goose River Press
3400 Friendship Road
Waldoboro ME 04572
e-mail: gooseriverpress@roadrunner.com
www.gooseriverpress.com

Dedication

These essays are dedicated to my grandfather,
Captain Charles Tozour, and to
my beloved parents, John and Belva Penn.

I owe a special thanks to Kelly Patton Brook, Joan
Hammer Grant, Carol Brightman, Ed Oestrich,
and my writing group, all who listened and
encouraged the work.

Preface

The coast is my history. It has shaped my past and defines the present in such a way that I cannot recall the events and people of my life without water as the context.

I grew up in a fading region of the Delaware bayshore and Atlantic coast, a landscape that now resides only in the cartography of my mind. I do not know why some memories are lost in the canvases of years, while others reside in finely detailed portraits, forever clear and unprofaned by age.

It is such memories that return to me now—a day long ago on my grandfather's oyster schooner, a coastal storm, my mother's death, an encounter with a whale on the coast of Maine—experiences that have all been circumscribed by water.

As I grow older it strikes me that the shore, in the limited perspective of my life, has been a place of fragile edges, both geological and personal, of beginnings and endings, of great joys and intense sorrows, of experiences that have given me an awareness of both the brevity and immensity of time. All of the stories in this book are about those layered, ephemeral boundaries at the interface of lives and events through which courses the presence of water.

Over the years, places and cherished faces have vanished, as fleeting as clouds reflected on the tidepools of a summer afternoon, but the stories help me to bring them back again, to remember. I hope the reader will find some humanity and a sense of wonder in all of them.

—Belva Ann Prycel
Sheepscot Village, Maine

Times and Tides

a memoir: essays of the coast

We are what suns, and winds and waters make us.
—George Savage Lander

dinghies on the bayshore

Port Norris

Sometimes when I visit the bayshores where I spent so much of my life, I find myself becoming lulled into an old nearly forgotten rhythm. The cadence of time is different there, like the motion of water, a gentler drawing down and returning, unlike the thrumming energy of ocean waters. And like the bay itself, I feel I may become again some part of a larger turning.

It is my spiritual landscape, a background of family and place, and a circular kind of migration that draws me there. The roots of it go deeper than the surfaces of buildings, villages, shorelines—for the certainty resides in me that on a level below my measurement and understanding I have been formed there—the product of winds and tides and ancestry extending far beyond my conscious memory.

And so it is when I travel the old marsh road into Port Norris, that I persist in seeing, not the vacant storefronts and distressed architecture of a depressed bayside community, but the graceful masts and tapered hulls, where in my memory, my grandfather still sails in the autumn wind.

I look at the sagging shucking houses, the empty chandleries and deserted docks, and I see instead the decks of schooners piled high in oysters, laborers shoveling the gleaming cargo, the shafts of filleting knives flashing silver on the water.

All of these images are anachronisms of another time, another day. But it is such a day that I recall in childhood,

1

and of a ship, the *Warfield*, with my broad-shouldered grandfather striding her decks. He is wearing a gray battered fedora and his tall form is encompassed in a dark jacket and vest. The implements of his trade rest around him—the giant claws of the dredge, heavy wooden cleats and pulleys, a varnished wheel and gimbolled brass compass, the massive vermicular coils of rigging and docklines nesting on the deck. I remember too the smells of decaying marshes, of gasoline and brine and the odors of the shucking houses upriver.

However, I was very young and could not know on that autumn day that he was selling his beloved ships, that the vessels, the piers, even the massively formidable figure of my grandfather were all as transient as the wispy vapors rising off the water and trailing voicelessly beside the hulls.

Such a day could not last, nor could the life of the baymen and the pursuit of a bivalve toward which so much passionate energy was directed. There was too much converging on that day, too much aggressiveness in the harvest, too much pollution, too much change. But it was not always so.

***

In the spring of 1905, the NJ Department of Shellfisheries listed 588 dredge boats like my grandfather's *Warfield* under sail in the Maurice River Cove area of New Jersey. At the turn of the century this fleet was said to be so numerous that "a man could walk on the hulls stretching from shore to shore,"* and it was not uncommon at oyster planting season for a forest of masts and miles of canvas to obliterate the view of the opposite bank.[1]

This was the vision, one still existing in old photos, of vessels resplendent at spring planting time, the season when the fleet raced up the bay to seed beds at the mouth of the Cohansey River. My grandfather's schooners— the *Warfield*, the *Jenny M. Chance*, the *Sherman*, and the *Newkirk*—were among those that coasted out the river, thousands of square feet of sail hoisted in the wind, rigging and cleats and lines all clamoring in an accompaniment to the day. The image was a symbol of the bay's bounty, but it was an image that was quietly dying even as the industry raced to ever greater exploitation.

In the early 1900's, bay watermen harvested as many as 25 million pounds of oysters a year from the bay bottom, and shucking houses lined the banks of tidal rivers, employing thousands of black packers and sorters. At the Port Norris docks alone, uncounted millions of oysters were shoveled off the decks of schooners and separated into graded piles of extras, primes, and cullings. A busy rail line serviced the docks where the oysters were shucked, packed, and hastily shipped on ice to lucrative urban markets.

Victorian palettes loved oysters, insistently demanded them, and so it was not surprising that during the harvest season the mounds of discarded oyster shells grew around the docks to the height of three and four-story buildings.

As the middens of shells rose higher, shipbuilding and supportive industries grew in tidal communities all along the bayshore. In towns like Greenwich, Dorchester, Leesburg, Bridgeton, Millville, and Mauricetown, skilled carpenters built a class of workboats still considered by many to be unequalled in versatility and beauty. Elegant wooden schooners and sloops, wide at the beam and with shallow drafts—proved perfectly suited to the bay waters. Like my grandfather's ships, they had retractable centerboards for skimming over shoals, a cabin with a galley, and beamy hulls adorned with a bowsprit or trailboard bearing the proud name of the vessel.

It was however, inevitable that this image of a bay festooned with majestic sails was not to last, for as early as the 1920's major technological advances were converting this fleet and the traditional manner of oyster harvesting into a new paradigm of industrial efficiency. Transitioning from dredging under sail, to the advent of large steam-powered dredges on the decks of dismasted schooners, introduced a level of technology never experienced on the bay before.

Some old watermen still lament that, "When they cut down the masts, they cut their throats." And in part that was true. Oystering was then free of the constraints of labor intensive techniques, no longer dependent upon the capricious winds and the subtle nuances of sail power, factors which had naturally tended to limit harvests in the past.

And with the onslaught of this new technology, the regenerative power of the oyster beds began to suffer. Profits tracked a slow decline from the 1920's through the Great Depression, when, in the midst of heavy industrialization and a burgeoning population, more ominous changes began to be seen on the bay.

***

It was always my family's custom on holidays to visit my mother's cousin Mina. A single schoolteacher, she was a loving yet fastidiously neurotic woman who rented an apartment near a civil war bastion on the Delaware called Fort Mott. Mina herself was something of a bastion of etiquette: a perfectionist, relentlessly controlling and precise. As such, our family visits were always proscribed by Mina's strict house rules and insistence on neatness and etiquette. During these times I often found escape in the company of two girls, oddly named Jackie and Billie, who lived below.

Together we scoured the banks of the river collecting driftwood, stones, and assorted debris, sometimes wading or swimming in the Delaware on hot summer days. Yet I discovered very early into these forays that it was necessary to bring an extra pair of sneakers for beach walking, for the Delaware River was, to put it mildly, one vast tarball. A can of kerosene was always kept by the backdoor of Mina's apartment for shoe cleaning, and Mina predictably kept her windows closed when the winds blew from the west, even on the hottest of days, so offensive were the odors from the oil refineries and chemical companies that spewed downriver.

But despite these olfactory assaults, Jackie liked to water ski, though she often developed nose and throat infections, and I suffered allergies that always seemed to worsen after a visit to Mina's. Though as children we never made the tenuous connection between the state of the Delaware and the state of our health. In those pre-environmental days, we accepted our afflictions as a part of life unrelated to the river.

However for the marine life of the Delaware, there was no such equivocation. Their world was irrevocably being poisoned, fouled, and smothered. Near the port of Philadelphia in the 1950's, dissolved oxygen levels were so despairingly low that even a marine worm could not survive. Shad could no longer pass the pollution block and reach the upper river to spawn, and fish kills were an annual occurrence. For some shipyard workers at the city docks, the smell of decaying marine life was often so intense that it was reported that hardy men would faint.

I suppose it is a miracle during this period that somehow, in the lower bay, oystering remained viable—although there too, the future was moving into troubled waters. No one completely saw it coming, but one of the last watermen to sell his business before the great collapse, was Charles "Cap" Tozour. Sadly, he could not know how fully and completely time was running out.

***

I recall that of all his attributes, my grandfather was a man who knew the importance of time. As a bay captain he reckoned with the confluence of rivers and bays and ocean currents, understood the phases of the moon and their mysterious effects on waves and tides, followed with a waterman's knowledge the shapes of clouds, and gauged when a bay storm could bounce off Bombay Hook and cross the

Delaware waters in a thunderous "bumper hooker." He understood intuitively the times when it was safe to leave port, and when it was prudent to stay in.

I remember he always kept a large gold watch on a chain tucked into his vest pocket, and he consulted it regularly. Everyday he appeared at our house promptly at 6PM to see me, his only granddaughter, then would leave considerately at 9PM when I went to bed.

In my earliest memories he was a presence in our home and I eagerly anticipated his visits each night, would sit on his lap while he told me stories, or sang to him all the new songs I had learned on the radio.

He bought me my first piano when I was three, an Acrosonic spinet which I still play regularly, and later, he built a house at the Jersey shore for my parents and me. These gifts he gave me in the short time I had with him, have echoed down through my life—gifts of joy that remain with me still.

At his residence in Millville, this generous and giving man of time had many clocks, but the most impressive was an antique wall clock mounted at the base of the stairs. On it was a reverse glass painting of a sailing ship heading out past a long promontory of land, piling cumulous clouds on the horizon, the wind filling the sails in a kind of 19th century romantic image of seafaring. It was appropriate for a bay captain, and it was this clock that chimed twice on the afternoon of December 22, 1950, as I stood with my Father in the quiet hallway. No one greeted us; no sounds of shuffling arthritic feet came from inside; only the click of a lock as my mother closed the door behind her, tears falling down her face. My grandmother came from the kitchen then, wiping her eyes with a linen handkerchief and leaning on her familiar cane.

In the afternoon, after selling the *Warfield* and his oyster business to a buyer from Delaware, my grandfather, Charles "Cap" Tozour, 72, had died of a heart attack.

His obituary stated: "Captain Charles Tozour, born in Delmont, died within a few weeks of his brother, Sherman. He was looked upon as one of the oldest, if not the oldest oyster boat owner and captain on the bay."

For my family, Christmas that year was an immeasurable sorrow, marked by hushed conversations and visits from people we rarely saw, bearing food instead of presents and condolences instead of Yuletide cheer. The funeral was just after Christmas Day and the whole experience seemed inappropriate to my child's mind, with festive wreaths and smiling Santas on lawns and porches while we were confronted with an enormity of loss. At the funeral, someone asked if I wanted to touch my grandfather's hands. They lifted me up to the coffin and I saw for the first time the certainty of death. My beloved grandfather's hands were white and cold, unlike the warm brown hands of the bay with the geography of his life written in their veins. I was only five, presumed too young to know such things, but I felt an immense sadness, a grief without words for expression.

Since that time, Christmas was always filled with melancholy, a hard time, especially for my mother. She kept a family Bible with the names of her father's boats inscribed inside, along with some photos and letters of family history. We had nothing tangible of the *Warfield* except these photos, and when I was in high school we learned it sank in a storm somewhere off the coast of Delaware.

It seemed then to my family that there was an inevitability in the crash that came to the oyster industry in 1957, seven years after my grandfather's death. It did not come, at least directly, from the over-fishing or pollution that was so apparent, but instead was embodied in the smallest of organisms, a mysterious parasite called multi-nucleated sphere X, (MSX). It attacked oysters in estuaries of the Atlantic Coast, killing off 90% of the oysters in the Delaware Bay. The following year, MSX moved into the lower Chesapeake where it spread destruction into Maryland waters. Since that time, despite research into disease-resistant oysters and environmental clean-up efforts, the oyster industry has never recovered.

For the vestigial fishery that remains, and for the disappearing Delaware Bay watermen, the memories of the glorious fleet under sail are rapidly fading.

I stand at the edge of a crumbling pier and I look back across the Bivalve docks, past the vacant buildings and skeletons of beached schooners—the rotting chine boards and ribs of the old oyster fleet—to the rolling bay with its silent legions of diseased mollusks. The present and the past blend subtly into a cold wintry light.

I drive home, crossing the Mauricetown causeway and over the meandering silver of the Maurice River. The old road goes beneath a new concrete bridge and ends at some depauperate piers where cakes of ice have sloughed and piled along the shoreline. A wintering oyster boat sits stoically in the mud, its silhouette stark against the backdrop of a profligately golding sky. The boat reminds me of the *Warfield* and that day with my grandfather so long ago.

If I strain very hard against the light, I think I can still see him there, a figure, hand on the wheel, foot braced against a gunnel. It happens a lot on the old road, the road into Port Norris.

But as I turn onto Route 47, and the busy highway leading back to my life in the North, I know I carry with me an ebb and flow of a different rhythm. It is a resonance of quieter waters, of change, and of loss. I cannot leave my history, nor ever choose to let it go, for it is my grandfather's legacy, written in a memory of autumn and outgoing tides.

---

[1]Under Sail by Donald Rolfs, Wheaton Historical Association, 1971.

winter evening by the river

For the animal shall not be measured by man. In a world older and more complete than ours, they move finished and complete, gifted with extensions of the senses we have lost or never attained, living by voices we shall never hear. They are...caught with ourselves in the net of life and time, fellow prisoners of the splendor and travail of the Earth.
—Edward Beston

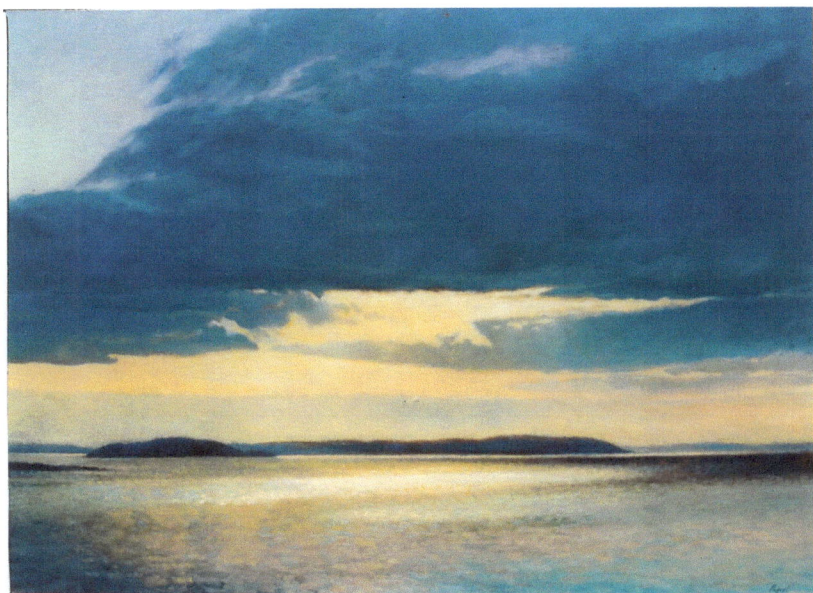

islands of Muscongus Bay

Whale

In November the northern landscape divests itself of the last remnants of the old year. White pines return their spent needles to the forest floor and grasses cast dried pockets of seeds to blow in the wind. Out along the coast the sedge bends in orange-tipped spears and breakers sculpt fractured rocks into polished crowns. Yesterday on my beach walk I picked up a handful of dried amber kelp and some large mussel shells of opalescent color. They sit in my studio, reminders of the sea but a few miles distant.

No matter what the season, my solitary walks always turn up something of value or give me some gift to carry home. Along the surfline I find the exoskeletons of sea creatures and the bleached armatures of animals. Colored pebbles and pearl-studded shells sift in the slurry of the tidepool, and broken nests of deserted eggs inhabit the ribs of dunes. Always at the sea edge, something is coming up, revealing itself, crossing the fluid borders of water and land. And sometimes, when least expected, the borders blur.

I think of this as I take the small wreath of sea lavender and descend the wooden steps to Ulins' Beach. The rocks of the tiny promontory stand stark and bare; the harbor shines in ruffled detachment. Yet I cannot feel so indifferent, for it was on this border that something came up once, and where I was privileged to have a strange meeting. It was not such a solitary event, for it echoed to one far back on a lost beach of my childhood. And it is there that I shall return.

***

"Mother, have you heard! A whale is on the beach!" I was breathless from running all the way from the lighthouse to our cottage four blocks away.

"A whale?" Mother asked incredulously. "Where?"

"Up by Uncle Bob's house. Hurry, we need to go!"

My mother was standing at the sink, peeling peaches, but seeing my excitement she threw off her apron and called to my father. The three of us hurried out the warped and banging screen door to the beach beyond.

News of the whale stranding must have spread quickly for a throng of people were gathered around a slumping gray form in the distance, something gigantic and dark, like a rounded circus tent, but foreign and massively out of context. My father said the whale was a humpback. It was motionless, belly down in the sand, beached midway between the foaming surfline and the highwater mark. When we arrived, people were futilely throwing buckets of water on a body the size of a small house. Yet the whale made no movement, no motion in that great sprawling form, and after several minutes I inched my way among the gathering of the curious till I stood at the head of this great creature. There I remained for what seemed like a long time.

In the kind of awe that only children can possess I marveled at such a wonder cast up from the sea, stared at the deep curved mouth, turned strangely down at the end, and then—abandoning my fear— I reached out and touched the skin, surprisingly soft. The eye, low on the head, seemed to be watching me. It was dark and round, like mine, I thought, but enormous and with a knowledge of a world I could barely conceive.

I knew the whale was dying, and I was a witness then as the light in the beautiful eye receded, the consciousness moving farther back and away till at last it was gone, a kind of filmy sheen replacing what had been there minutes before.

16

Around me talk dissolved into silence; people speaking in whispers.

But then the others soon came—men with saws. In an act that I could only perceive as a kind of consummate sacrilege they began sawing away at the 40-foot carcass, disassembling the whale piece by piece before it could putrefy in the sun.

I watched in horror as the first cube of white-pink blubbery flesh peeled away, then left in tears.

That summer I was possessed by thoughts of whales, dreams of encounters in the ocean as I drifted on my canvas raft, floating beyond the breakers in an empty sea. In some internalized way the whale had confirmed by its existence the immensity of the ocean of which I had been childishly unaware. Something had come up from the waters and held me in its dark eye, along with an intimation of all that was unknown in those depths, all that was unfathomable.

There were other things to come up from the depths that year when a northeast storm rumbled up the coast and the troubled sea disgorged piles of conches, giant spider crabs, and four-foot dunes of surfclams onto the beach. Among this debris, an ancient bone, a weathered whale vertebrae, lay amid the decaying clams and orange popping kelp. Doggedly, I pushed and dragged the bone along the edge of the rackline, half rolling, half carrying it to our back porch where it remained for many years as a makeshift stool and object of general curiosity. There I would sit on rainy days, thinking of whales and weaving necklaces of plastic beads then stringing clam shells with bore holes as ornaments. In the background were always the susurrant waves, beating their insistent percussion, and I imagined whales riding the ocean currents to this thrumming, surfacing and plunging, very deep and far out.

Although the image of the whale persisted for a very long time, as a child I could not perceive the intelligence and sensibilities of the creature that had died on that long distant

17

beach, but I knew however that my sense of the world, and my measurement of it, had forever changed. In this way, and others much harder to define, the whale of my youth never left me. Something in his dying eye touched a nine-year-old girl, and even in death his power remained. I could not know it then, but it would be fifty years before I met another of his kind, and it would be in a tiny harbor, far to the north.

***

"Looks like a fine sailin' day, yep," the whistling man in the sweaty tee-shirt and Greek fisherman's cap addressed me as he headed up the pier.

"Uh-huh," I replied mindlessly.

A few cormorants floated listlessly on Round Pond Harbor, and across Muscongus Bay the hazy outline of Loud's Island hung disembodied above a smoky sea.

I watched as my husband Lew maneuvered our small sloop around a phalanx of lobster boats and then headed toward my pickup point at the town dinghy dock. It was a quiet morning and my eyes unfocused, meandering over the little harbor while a resident herring gull picked mussels from an encrusted fishing pier. Yes, it should be a good day, I thought, watching the breeze just beginning to ruffle the water slightly, grateful for an auspicious sailing wind. And it was then that an odd motion caught the periphery of my vision—something that flashed on the water, a dark shape that arched and disappeared directly behind our boat. I blinked, unsure of what I had seen, a shining ripple the only indicator of a movement so implausible that I immediately questioned whether I had imagined it.

Perhaps a seal? They often come into the harbor, particularly when the mackerel are running. But no...it seemed too large...

I looked at Lew, who was oblivious to my observation, and oddly preoccupied with the engine, but I began to feel a

Round Pond lobster boat by Loud's Island

prescient and prickly sense of anxiety.

The feeling did not diminish as Lew prematurely cut the engine and bumped the pilings in an inexplicably awkward docking uncharacteristic of his seamanship skills. He was straining backwards over the stern, hanging, balanced over the engine, a deep puzzlement written across his face.

Under the wake of the boat I could barely make out the object of his concern—a huge shape trailing the hull, a shadow obscured in a mass of bubbles directly beneath the rotating propeller blades.

We both peered warily into the dissipating prop wash, astonished to see a "fish," approximately ten feet long, its eyes distinctly visible, looking up at us.

"It followed me all the way in from the mooring," Lew said. "I don't know what the heck it is...."

I leaned farther over the pier for a better view but the huge animal vanished under the hull, leaving our boat wobbling and a heavy thunk emanating from somewhere below the surface.

"Wh-what in the w-world do you think..." I began, but suddenly my words were cut short as a massive gray shape erupted next to the pier, exploding in a volley of spray and wetting my Bean Bag and the surrounding dock with saltwater. A huge circular wake radiated outward, rocking the dinghies in an abrasive groaning and tug of lines.

"Whoa...what's that?" the man with the Greek sailors cap called suddenly from behind me, scratching a bald spot above his plastered gray fringe of hair.

"I don't know...a porpoise...?" I trailed off indecisively.

"Nah, not a porpoise." I thought he looked like a local, both condescending and a little amused. "Naaaah, not a porpoise," he said again, drawing out the words as if to confirm his verdict. "Looks more like some kinda whale...maybe that young bee-luga that's been spotted acrost' bay in Portland...lost its mother and been hangin' arount hahbahs."

I had never heard of whales "hangin' arount hahbahs"

before, certainly never gotten close enough to be sprayed by one. But whatever the explanations, the whale seemed disinterested in our speculations, for he was heading off, bent upon intimidating an old man rowing a dory, now paddling much faster than previously thought possible.

We took advantage of the distraction and slipped lines. Lew restarted the engine, and I went forward to sit on the edge of the cabin. I was feeling unsettled, certainly more than a little perplexed by this strange wayward cetacean. What was a whale doing in the harbor anyway? And why had he been so interested in our boat? I had never heard of whales chasing dories or cruising under propellers before. What had just happened here?

Perhaps as fate would have it—or maybe because we were the only large moving object on the harbor that day—my musings were short-lived, for when I glanced back I saw a familiar figure bounding and rolling up in our wake, assuming his old position directly under the dangerous propeller blades.

Alarmed, Lew slapped his hand hard on the side of the hull. The shadowy figure did not move. Lew slapped again, several hard thumps, and our companion disappeared under the keel.

We both waited, exchanging worried glances as Lew kept the engine barely idling. Silence. Then seconds later I nearly lost my perch on the forward rail as a geyser of water shot up next to the bow.

Wet now, I clumsily clawed my way along the handrail, looking down into the water where I saw our friend wedged into the contour of the hull, almost snuggling the boat. He was moving in perfect synchronicity with our speed. A pink blowhole with its accompanying cloud of vapor haloed his head, and water rippled over a series of old slash marks on his back—probable wounds from encounters with propellers. His tail, in another form of entanglement I presumed, bore a small v-shaped notch. In a moment, he disappeared again, only to resurface once more next to the dangerous rotating blades.

Now it was I who began thumping the hull, feeling protective—he was swimming with us after all—and he soon returned to the bow, washing me in a grateful exhalation of whale spray, misting my clothes and the surrounding deck with seawater. Again I peered down into darkness, and again he was gone. Again, I frenetically resumed my banging, and again, he returned. This bizarre scenario of attraction and withdrawal played out repeatedly as we neared the mouth of the harbor.

I should state here that Round Pond harbor, at its salty entrance to Muscongus Bay, is a nearly un-navigable sea of lobster buoys—a bobbing obstacle course of markers and traplines. Lew struggled to navigate this maze while being watchful of our strange companion. I helplessly flattened myself, wet, on the forward deck and waited. I didn't have to wait long for the shadowy figure soon emerged again, but this time directly under me.

I felt a certain twinge of anticipation then, a fey sense that something was about to happen, although nothing could have fully prepared me for what followed.

Rolling slightly on his side, the whale curiously eyed me. I watched, befuddled, as he casually lifted his head, playfully bumping a small plastic boat fender dangling off a cleat. All the while his eyes never left me.

Astounded I lay on the whale-washed deck. A small breeze lifted up from the bay, playing in the rigging and making a tiny bell-like sound that seemed to come from some undefined space and distance. Up ahead the harbor yawned into a widening expanse of blue and a freshening wind pressed against the hull. In that moment the waters of the Atlantic fetched down the Gulf of Maine, and something lost and remembered called in the heart.

I reached my hand down into the water. I know, looking back, I did not examine risk, and I had no expectations, but

I felt he too was reaching out in some way.

It was then that he began to rise, floating like a leaf to the surface, moving closer, his eyes never leaving me—until suddenly I felt my hand resting on top of a scarred head. What motivated him to do this, I will never fully know, any more than I will understand what led me to reach down to him, but I think there was loneliness in it, and time. Saltwater trickled across my lips and stung my eyes. We were swimming together then, heading out to the open sea.

Too quickly it seemed, as all wonders must pass, on that magical day this too ended. A noisy lobster boat artlessly clambered by, its great rumbling engine creating a gurgling, grumbling vibration and he left me then, seduced by other voices, but I felt he was looking for something and I hoped he would find his way home. The last sight I had of him was a flick of a tail as he swam away in pursuit of something he could not name, and to a place where I could not follow.

***

The wind of November rises up the hill, chafing the bare branches and I look again on the harbor. Three months have passed, and in their passage I learned of a mysterious young beluga whale named Poco, an animal described by researchers as a "solitary sociable". Poco lost his pod somewhere in the waters of Nova Scotia and had developed a strange compensatory and unusually unguarded interest in humans. The researchers I spoke with noted that he was particularly attracted to the sounds of engines, noises vaguely reminiscent of the murmurings and bubbling communications of his whale companions. In the solitude of the North Atlantic, he had wandered far south, out of the territory of other belugas, and he was lost in a friendless, voiceless sea.

This may have been why he joined us on that August day, but I really do not believe that was the sum of it, any more than "solitary sociable" explains the immensity of his reaching out. I prefer to think that we were two travelers who shared an act of communion on a long journey.

In November, Pocos' body washed ashore in South Portland, Maine. The researchers quickly came to claim it, to autopsy and probe with probably no less compassion in their scientific need for knowledge than the men who had disassembled a whale on that beach so long ago. I did not inquire as to the reason for his death. He had gone, and I was merely impoverished for his passing.

I will remember him as I look out over the waters of Round Pond Harbor, chasing dories and glistening with reckless life. I am honored, beyond any achievement of my humble life, that I was here once, when he came up to touch me across a boundary greater than time. He was named Poco, and he was a whale that swam with me.

I place the small wreath of sea lavender on the water and watch it gently wobble and rock in the current, then slowly move out with the tide.

This was my last journey to the sea before the long winter set in.

The wind was a noreaster, blowing squally off the sea;
And cliffs and spouting breakers were the only things a-lee.
— Robert Louis Stevenson

Muscongus Bay, morning storm

Storms

It seems to me there's an odd sound the wind makes in the hours before storms, a certain uneasy absence as a vacuum where the air is withdrawn then released in little gustings that fuss around the eaves and cause the multiflora rose bushes to scratch irritably against the clapboards.

Last night the weather forecasters predicted three days of rain. A hurricane is slogging up the coast and we are feeling the first squalls spawned by the huge low pressure system to our south. In the last hour the barometer has dropped precipitously and storm clouds have closed the remaining loopholes of blue into a solid tent of gray.

To those attuned to it, the wind always speaks of change, reveals itself in intermittent quiverings that make the house vibrate while crickets emit a high-pitched sustained note only heard before storms. Out on the harbor, long flights of gulls coast in from the bay. I put on the coffee pot and instinctively draw some pans of water.

In the southern part of New Jersey in the 50's and 60's, we were always recovering from, or bracing for, another storm. These appeared in the form of hurricanes or northeasters that rumbled up the coast leaving rough waters, flooding, or sometimes destruction in their wake.

The first storm to impress itself on my young consciousness was in 1950. It was also in this storm that I saw my father perform a feat of incredible daring or recklessness, depending upon one's personal disposition and view of such things. However, as a child I bore no judgment at the time; I was merely an observer, left with my mother and grandfather standing on the bank of an overpass beside a flooded coastal marsh.

Where I watched that day was over a mile from the coast, looking at a sea of unfamiliar white-capped breakers extending out to the barrier island of Sea Isle. A thin line of houses peered above the waters where I knew land should have been, and leaning telephone poles and sagging power lines formed the only demarcation of a road, a pathetic cordon that disappeared like matchsticks in the watery landscape.

My father stood on the overpass, reflecting on the incredible scene. Then I watched as he cut a walking stick from a sapling by the highway and announced that he was going to follow the telephone poles till he reached the island.

"I know I can get out there. I want to check the house," he said determinedly.

At this absurdly brave or desperately foolhardy announcement my mother became vehement in her opposition, declaring she would rather lose a house than a husband.

"John, are you *nuts*? Nobody's out there. Nobody's going to save you if you drown. Of all the dumb stunts...who cares about the house?"

My mother did not spare words when she was angry, but her anger this day was sorely matched by my father's innate stubbornness.

"Look, I'll go now on the low tide. I'll be back before it turns." Then as an afterthought... "I have my stick." He waved the stick like a saber, slicing the air around him ridiculously.

"Dammit, John, you're going to get yourself killed. You think that stick's gonna save you?"

My father didn't hear the rest of her objections for he was already on his way, scrambling down the New Jersey Parkway overpass, trudging through the first shallow breakers. Foolhardy or brave, hero or clown, etched in my memory is his figure, small and dark in the distance, thigh deep in water, moving with his walking stick, testing for potholes and washouts on the submerged road.

All through the afternoon we waited. I stayed close to my mother on the top of the overpass and we held our vigil while the winds continued to blow steadily out of the northeast and until the tide began to swell up the edges of the parkway. I suppose my mother and grandfather watched it creep up the embankment as one watches seawater filling the hold of a sinking ship, each wave signaling some diminishment of hope, some greater urgency and despair.

My grandfather stoically, and transparently untruthfully, tried to assure my mother that everything would be all right. Of course she didn't believe him and her anxiety just compounded during the waning hours.

I recall it was sometime in late afternoon that we saw a movement far off along the power lines, a small spot at first, but one that became a smudge, then a smudge that became a line, then a small unwinding ribbon of people moving hand in hand, arm in arm, a human chain inching slowly toward the land. As the procession moved closer, I could see my father at the head of the group, his walking stick still before him, leading his people like Moses to the safety of the Promised Land.

Soon a tide of grateful souls, wet but smiling as people do who have survived a great ordeal, gathered on the overpass. They were all shaking hands with my father, and I believe my mother forgot her anger then.

Although no paper reported it, and no credit was ever given, my father was the first person to enter the flooded town of Sea Isle, the only person to rescue stranded people that day.

By some act of amazing good fortune our summer cottage survived the 1950 storm. And so by a larger miracle did my father. But this was just a first lesson in my father's courage—and the ocean's staggering power. There would be many other lessons to follow.

***

My Uncle Bob was a shipyard worker who spent all of his life around water. In his youth he worked on Delaware Bay dredge boats as a deckhand, and after World War II, where he served in North Africa, he returned home to work in the boat-building trades as a caulker—or a "corker" as he liked to say.

When I was a teenager, I viewed my Uncle Bob as a roguish figure, six feet tall with a lanky frame topped in a shock of bright red hair and possessed of a charmingly devilish manner. He laughed with his whole body in a shaking, snuffling, snort of a laugh, and among his many wildly endearing qualities he shared my fascination for water. During gales and heavy storms I would often find him at the top of the dunes, "sniffing the salt" as he would say, holding back his head with the requisite doglike snort in the face of a good blow, glorying in the power of storm waves and riptides.

It was on such a day that I found him clinging tenaciously to the crest of a dune at the end of our street, his shirt and pants flapping wildly. It was a noisily dramatic day, violent with the passage of Hurricane Carol a hundred miles off the coast. Foam blew up the beach and over the top of the dune, skipping and flying down the street, then cascading over the highway to lodge in the tall marsh beyond. This was no ordinary foam such as one finds dwindling at the end of common breakers dissipating on a beach. It was the output of a huge churning monster of a tropical low many nautical miles out in the North Atlantic, the kind of foam so dense and deep that I imagined storm-wrecked boaters could suffocate in its depths as they helplessly waited for rescue.

I dodged airborne missiles of suds the size of giant sofa cushions being hurled overhead and leaned against the

32

whiplashing wind blowing at 50 or 60 knots. My clothes slapped my skin painfully, and the force of the gusts made my eyes ache in their sockets. Leaning forward I tried once to fall over, and could not do it.

When I reached Uncle Bob we didn't speak. Any words would have been carried away in the roar of crashing breakers, and there was nothing particularly relevant to say anyway. The sight was too terrifying, the coastline too utterly transformed into a battlezone of sucking undertows and 20-foot steep-sided walls of water, yawning and groaning and crumbling in on themselves as they smashed to shore. But with the fearful crashing there was a more disturbing element, a kind of sonorous undertone, like an alto growl just beneath the screech-pitched tenor of the wind. It frightened me more than the sight of the waves themselves, and I shuddered to think that only a day ago I had surfed this sea now transformed into the raging stuff of nightmares.

Back at the cottage my mother nervously stirred a pot of clam chowder, cooking as she always did in a time of crisis, watching from the kitchen window, worrying that we should have evacuated to the mainland hours ago. Yet the weather reports had been so benign, so insignificant, that we were unprepared for the ferocity of the storm.

Uncle Bob and I, chilly and battered, sat down to bowls of the warm chowder at the old clawfoot kitchen table. But we had barely begun to eat when around us noisily reverberated clashes and clangs and a tearing of wood and metal, the sounds of unsecured objects and building parts breaking away in the havoc outside. We all ran to the living room and stood agape as our neighbor's new vinyl porch roof peeled off and became airborne. Simultaneously a nearby carport tore away and skidded toward the marsh.

With that my father decisively announced, "That's it. We're leaving!" But his announcement had little effect. It was too late. Water was already pouring around the dunes and racing down the street in salty rivers. We were caught in a storm surge then and there was nowhere to go.

The house grew silent. I had no more appetite for the chowder.

We were stranded on the first floor, something I considered soberly as I contemplated the tiny trap door leading to the attic. My father's boat, a wooden Lyman, sat on its trailer inside the garage. We couldn't reach it now, so at that dire moment we simply huddled together, expecting to see water pressing under the door or seeping up through the floorboards. The initial excitement of watching the hurricane had disappeared, replaced by fear. My parents vowed they would never again trust weather reports. We all cursed the local weatherman for his ineptitude.

Uncle Bob remained peering out the window, rocking back and forth on his heels, arms folded tightly against his body. My mother put her arm about my shoulders, telling me we would somehow get through this, her eyes filled with fear. My father, more inclined to action in a crisis, grabbed some flotation gear and inner tubes from a back closet and was pulling down the folding stairs leading to the attic.

But in the midst of this scene, as if a switch on a giant fan had been pulled, the screech-pitched tenor of the wind seemed to subtly alter. We stopped and listened, hearing the tone shift from a shriek to a slightly minor wolflike howl. Over the next few minutes the howl descended in scale to a moan, followed a few minutes later by a gusty swooshing sound at the windows. At the last there was only a sense of displacement, as a freight train that passes, leaving a tangible echo, then a silence.

Within an hour that day the tide turned and receded to the lowest point that people ever remembered. It exposed old mudflats, pilings, and traces of vanished buildings never seen before. As the sun pierced the last clouds and brilliant sunshine returned, only the puddles and debris hinted at the horror of the past few hours.

With the changing of the tide, we too left, shaken. We

never stayed through another hurricane, no matter how reassuring the weather predictions. Our trust in all prognostication was broken and we were ecstatically happy to have survived.

Surely no one could have known it then, but this was just a preview of storms to come and the worst disaster to hit the Atlantic coast in a generation, the Great Storm of '62. It began as an unremarkable northeaster, but when it had ended, our lives would be forever changed.

***

The summer cottage on 28th Street, the joy of my childhood, was built by my grandfather in the spring of 1948, given to my parents "for the little girl who loved water," he said. It was a simple unadorned beach house with green asbestos shingle siding, a wide front porch lined with creaky rockers, an open kitchen and living room, an inside bath and an outdoor coldwater shower. My mother heated water for bathing using a whistling teakettle on the propane kitchen stove. Rainwater was caught in an open barrel, warmed by the sun, and this gave us the illusion of a heated shower, however briefly. Tall foxtails grew to the back of the house, and I would lay on my bed in the morning and watch redwinged blackbirds gather in the grasses. My friends, Richard, Billy and Joanne built hideaways in the marsh grass and made driftwood forts in the shady protection of dunes.

Across the street lived Smitty and his wife Carrie, a rough-spoken, portly, good-natured couple who came only on weekends and made spaghetti with crabs in a pot that seemed the size of a factory boiler. Whenever we saw them, they were always in the process of catching the crabs, boiling the pasta, or making the red sauce to garnish it all. They affectionately called me "Bell," and they had a strange little Chihuahua named Tootsie—pale, nearly hairless, and perpetually quivering, who sat on the table with her bottom on the silverware and ate from Smitty's hand or off his plate. My immaculately clean mother was appalled at this, but she would make us all join Smitty for the requisite pasta as she did not want to offend. After every meal at Smitty's there would be music on the radio—Frankie Avalon, Brenda Lee, and Pat Boone—then I would scurry home to wash my hands and scour my mouth with Listerine.

Next door to Smitty lived the mysterious and glamorous Mrs.Harvey. She came from "the city" and no one seemed to know very much about her, although I fantasized she must have had some kind of theatrical career, with her dark glasses and Esther Williams figure. Two blocks south of us lived my best summer friend, Jerry Rae, and on the corner were Billy and Donny and Joanne, all cousins from Philadelphia, and my beach pals whose large extended family crowded in noisy profusion and perpetual argument their grandmother's summer house.

But most significantly, just a block away, and easily visible from our front porch...was the home of Richard, my first love from the age of six until puberty, my childhood companion of the tidepools. Every morning, Richard would sit on our back porch and sing out in mock proper English, "Cheerio, Belva Ann," then together we would disappear for the day at the beach, returning only for dinner after creating adventures on sea and sand.

Richard and I built sandcastles, surfed waves, crabbed in tidepools, and played ball or "clamshoes," our version of horseshoes using clam shells tossed into holes. We invented highwire acts balanced on posts and bulkheads or straddling the narrow concrete remains of the lighthouse barricade, poised over breaking waves.

On rainy days, we were joined by Joanne and Billy on the back porch, and together made necklaces out of plastic beads, or fashioned plaster of Paris paper weights, enshrining all our best seashell finds into immortal stone. Evenings we could be found haunting the boardwalk, the smell and sounds of which can be instantly summoned today despite a passage of half a century—a blend of popcorn, cotton candy, hotdogs, sea salt, waves breaking on the pilings, the organ grinder-like music of the carousel, and a sense of anticipation for something unknown.

The most romantic part of the boardwalk was the Madeleine, an elegant old movie theatre on pilings that projected far into the ocean at high tide. At the Madeleine one could sit in the plush velvet seats and watch romantic adventures as the waves broke lustily beneath the floor. My first serious kiss was in the Madeleine, followed by a long moonlit walk home with Richard, barefoot and breathless.

Lastly, just five short blocks up the beach from our cottage, Uncle Bob and Aunt Mary Emma had a summer house, and just beyond them, my mother's cousin Mina spent weekends at her father's place on Whale Beach, the site of the strange and tragic whale stranding.

All of this made up a context of life and lives that embodied the shore far beyond mere physical characteristics, a web of relationships that grew over time and formed the basis of an extended family and community.

**

There was nothing in the weather reports that early spring day to suggest anything unusual. On March 5th, 1962, our local TV meteorologist, whom we poetically called "Wally Kinnan the Weatherman," noted that there was a "high level low" coming up from the Carolinas, with probable clearing by afternoon.

But on the following day, March 6th, the first distress calls began coming in from Long Beach Island. The radio reported thirty-foot waves pounding the beach and breaching dunes. That same day, farther up the coast, a US Navy destroyer, the *USS Monssen* washed ashore in Holgate. Elsewhere, similar reports began to fill the airwaves. In

Atlantic City, a barge crashed into the Steel Pier, taking out a 350 foot section; the Steel Pier water tank used by the famous diving horse was dislodged by waves and swept south where it destroyed the Ventnor Fishing Pier; in Stone Harbor, water crashed over the tops of beachfront houses; and in Sea Isle, the first high tide took out the boardwalk and the *Madeleine.*

It was sometime on the afternoon of the third day that my parents and I drove to the coast and returned to the infamous overpass near Route 9 where twelve years before I had watched my father disappear into a desolate waste. Using his inferior binoculars, my father reported that he could not see the summer cottage, nor any of those around it on 28th Street,—and that my uncle's house and the whole of Whale Beach appeared to be gone.

A day later the winds finally ceased. The length of the Jersey shore lay in ruins. Damage estimates from Virginia to New England ranged in the hundreds of millions of dollars, a staggering sum for the 1960s. In New Jersey alone, 4000 homes were destroyed. Ours was one of them.

***

We walked among fields of debris, seeing nothing familiar but the street signs. The National Guard allowed us to return to the old neighborhood where just one recognizable structure remained, probably the poorest built of dwellings but one which had miraculously been spared the battering of other houses floating and breaking up in the waves. My parent's house was moved but intact, relocated across the street, in the marsh, where it partially blocked the southbound lane of the main highway. When wrecking crews arrived to clear the road we had little time to rescue household items, but my parents tried to box the few remaining items they could salvage.

I recall that a foot of sand covered our kitchen floor as my fastidious mother packed Willow Ware plates. The refrigerator was gone. It took three men to move it into the kitchen when new, with a mere quarter inch of clearance through the back door. Somehow during the storm it had exited the house through the same door while leaving everything else intact. My grandmother's settee and the clawfoot table remained and were salvaged, and in one of those incomprehensible oddities that victims of storms are fond of noting, the salt and pepper shakers and glass containers on the open shelves in the kitchen, sat undamaged where we had left them. But my prized whalebone, found in another coastal storm, was gone, returned to the sea.

I left my mother to her packing and walked up the beach toward the direction of Uncle Bob's house, lost in the surreal landscape. Amid a sea of wreckage, far out in the former marsh, I saw Bob's tan Volkswagen, squatting on the hard sand near Ludlams' Bay, close to the site of his old clamming spot. Part of a building was deposited there along with fabric, boards, broken furniture, and random roofs and walls. I recognized some of this as the back portion of Uncle Bob's house. The door miraculously remained, and stupidly, as there was no back wall or any windows, I knocked.

Aunt Mary Emma was "inside," folding a soggy rag that she informed me was her treasured lobster tablecloth, neatly squaring the cloth as I'd seen her do a hundred times after a breakfast of Sunday morning pancakes. The whole scene was ridiculous and I started to laugh hysterically. Then suddenly we both began to cry.

"Gone," she said, shaking her head, "all gone."

***

This was all a long time ago, and after so many years, it seems to me, that the loss of a beach house should not be such an important thing. It was, after all, just an object...so much timber and plaster. Replaceable. But what was not so replaceable were the associations one makes, the patchwork of life and memories one imprints into the wood and fabric and bones of a house, the people who were part of the landscape of the house, the place that formed the greater territory of the spirit and mind, and those never to be repeated moments in time.

We never replaced the summer house that my grandfather built, and my enchanted childhood at the coast came to an abrupt end.

It was then, as a teenager, after the storm of '62 that I learned the cost of living on the coast is the price of loss that can never be equated in dollars and cents, in insurance estimates or replacement values. It's a human toll, and it runs deep. I think of this whenever I hear an announcement of a northeaster, or of a distant hurricane building somewhere in the depths of the Caribbean. I am still reminded in the smell of popcorn, the gleam of a Willow Ware plate, or the snuffling irritable little sounds the wind makes before storms. It all comes back in the smallest of things, "the remembrance of things past... that lingers," as Proust said, "like souls."[1]

I look apprehensively out the window of my Maine cottage and turn to pour a cup of coffee from the kettle. The wind shakes the house and continues its rattling at the eaves. Out on the harbor, boats tug restlessly at their moorings, and a ship's bell sounds from somewhere on Muscongus Bay. There is no stopping it. It always comes back...the faces, the coast, the years. I see it all again, see *them* all again.

And this I remember in storms.

---

[1] *A Remembrance of Things Past* by Marcel Proust, Nantier Beall Minoustchine Publishing, 2003.

The marsh, to him who enters it in a receptive mood, holds, besides mosquitoes and stagnation, melody, the mystery of unknown waters, and the sweetness of Nature undisturbed by man.
—Charles William Beebe

Bayside fishing shack

The Marsh

I have been told, by people one presumes to know such things, that there are few places as elemental or mysterious as a great salt marsh. I believe this is true, for much of my adult life I lived beside one, a verdant pelt of vegetation that bordered the turbid Delaware Bay.

The treasures from that area were vast, a heritage of colonial villages along tidal tributaries, bayside outposts and fishing communities, sandy beaches and fertile farm fields.

It was there in 1986, in the village of Greenwich, that I set up a studio in a 1730 farmstead. I was in my forties, married, and working as an artist and teacher and I began to paint the light of the luminescent bayshore skies. I worked mostly out of doors, alone, under the mysterious refracting haze of those skies. And it was also there, I believe, that I began to perceive the presence of miracles.

Perhaps "miracles" is a word that few would use these days, but for me there is no other term for events that have retained such a power and force over the years.

I suppose it all began in September, in the autumn, when red berries first appeared on the scraggly bushes beside a marsh lane and the leaves of the swamp maples were just beginning to pick up traces of burgundy and gold. It was a time that I liked to meander along a little unpaved road, one that skirted a forest and ended in a broad marsh beside the tidal Cohansey River. Along this road, interspersed among the phragmites and cordgrasses, were islands of tall cedar trees created by native Americans whose middens of oyster shells had elevated the soil, allowing upland vegetation to flourish. I stopped beside one of these islands, intending a small respite from my walk.

As I entered the leafy coolness, with the cedars towering high above me, remote and dark, it was cathedral-like, quiet; I heard nothing but the crunch of my shoes on the brittle branches of the forest floor. Overhead, in the dark viridian of the trees, nested a tapestry of orange leaves, a network of vines and tangled color lacing the branches. I looked absently about, flicking my walking stick among the grasses, observing nothing—when suddenly, without warning, the woods exploded.

A sudden burst of power, a buffeting of air, of wings, swirled about my face and hair, beating in alarm. In the heights above, thousands of leaves erupted in animated flight.

I froze, too startled to move, a blundering intruder, a trespasser in some vast undertaking of which I had been previously ignorant. I had disturbed a secret, a solitary place of communion—of Monarchs.

I stood, silent, and gradually the wild beating ceased. The Monarchs settled, returning one by one to the trees, flexing their wings in a repetitive motion that reminded me of hands assuming a position of prayer. Then I slowly backed away, inching toward the light of the marsh lane from which I had come.

***

This was an initiation of sorts, but I was about to learn that the marsh there teemed with all manner of life, and all forms of surprise. And it was, perhaps, my solitary lot as a plein air painter, that I found myself in places to encounter it on its own terms, and often on the same isolated marsh road of which I now write.

Greenwich Marsh

A fellow landscape painter, Al Nicholson, used to speak of the marshes there as "full of spirit," and of the light as "transcendent, lambent." I loved Al; I loved his spirit, his feel for the landscape and the light. And it was, I recall, in pursuit of this spiritual light that I often brushed upon things unexpected, as I did one afternoon when I set up my easel not far from some crab shacks at the end of the lane. A shower had just passed and the marsh grass glistened with the washing of the cleansing rain. The sky too was clearing, just turning that premonitory shade of violet that was the promised compensation for an excessively torrid summer day. I busied myself, scraping around on my palette, smearing alizarin crimson and cobalt blue among the mottled paints in preparation for catching some rosy hues of sunset color.

I was probably so focused on the task at hand that I failed to notice the ground around me. Or maybe it was the clicking noise that ultimately alerted me—like the sound of thousands of tiny scissors clipping grass, but I looked up to see a strange undulation of the marsh. I say "of the marsh" because there was not a single spot "in" the marsh that caught my attention; rather it was the movement of the *totality* of the marsh itself. I looked about, stunned, to see a wave of black fiddler crabs—millions of them—cropping the grass for acres around, gleaning the fresh detritus carried in from the bay—and I was squarely in the center of their exodus.

Frankly until that time I had previously only seen fiddlers in small colonies along the tidal creeks and was utterly unaware that they were the marsh's most prolific resident—with a population that could exceed a million per acre. I certainly had never heard of anyone being surrounded by a sea of them on a marsh road.

Slowly the black wave approached, every outsized claw raised in rage, every giant chiloped shaking in unison and defiance at the odd invader in their midst. It was a threatening study in malevolence, and I had the surreal image of being devoured by a mass of angry fiddlers where I stood, but the black army mercifully parted just a few feet away, circling and raging, flowing like a dark noisy river. I don't know how long it took for that clanking, clangorous throng to pass by, but I knew I would never see fiddlers in quite the same way again. I packed my paints and beat a hasty retreat to the studio.

In the years afterwards, I sometimes saw small troops of fiddlers in the woods behind our barn, and once even found two suspiciously cowering in a corner of the basement—yet I never met anyone—neither crabber, nor artist, nor fisherman—who seems to have experienced anything quite like my encounter.

Of course there were other residents of the fields and salt meadows—ghosts—fleeting white phantoms that emerged at night. They were the barn owls.

For years a family of them sheltered in the rafters of the great barn behind our house, raising their young in a box near the peak of the tall roof. The researchers who came each year to study them sometimes slept in the barn, waiting for a capture and a banding as the owls began their nightly foragings.

It was a strange time with these nightly visitors, both human and avian. The scientists were an amiably odd group, like the barn owls themselves, accustomed to working in the dark, waiting hours without moving on ladders or uncomfortable cots, positioned beside hollow trees or under creaky barn rafters.

The owls were a wily lot too, alert for any sign of movement, their night vision finely tuned for any hint of predator or prey. So these captures became a kind of annual contest between two clever species, and we watched it all with a sense of fascination. We also came to know the owls very well.

The owls likewise came to know us, although our first meeting was terrifyingly memorable. It occurred right after we moved into the Greenwich house, after an exhausting dawn to dusk effort. I needed a change of scene, was drained, and walked into the huge yard between the house and barn to look at the brilliantly clear night sky. There was no moon and no ambient light to intrude on the immense darkness. The stars, astoundingly intense, fell all the way to the edge of the horizon.

It was a magnificent night, and I was placidly looking up when a bone-chilling shriek broke the silence. A huge white form came gliding toward me, passing barely six feet above my head, its wings extended and a frightening white face peering down.

Nearly falling backward, I reclaimed my footing and watched in awe as the phantom figure circled over the house then made another pass at me, higher this time, shrieking fiercely again. By then my husband heard the commotion and joined me. We both watched as the ghostly owl circled several more times then disappeared into the cavernous interior of the barn. All was silent.

"You were a stranger, and he didn't know you," said one of the researchers when I told them the story later. Of course they were right. I was on the owl's territory, and not the other way around. I needed to be examined, studied, which I was.

Following that experience there were no more frightening shrieks of alarm, no more engagements except of the most respectful kind—those of two creatures co-habitating the same property and going about their respective business. At night I would sometimes see the pale owl messengers coming and going, or hear their chattering young when I passed under the owl box, but I felt we maintained a gracious and mutual kind of acknowledgment and acceptance.

Certainly there were other visitations, the annual migrations of snow geese whose wintry appearances were a thing of beauty, blanketing the fields and marshes in dense throngs like drifts of pure white snow, springtime migrations of horseshoe crabs so prolific that they piled like animated boulders on the bayshore, visitations of swallows arriving

afternoon sky, Greenwich Marsh

from Mexico on exactly the 17th day of every May, and once a gathering of fireflies on a summer evening—a host of thousands that packed so tightly they lighted the forest behind them in an eerily reflected glow, moving, synchronized, as one organism.

I consider these things now as all part of the common miracles. Today whenever I cross the great marsh on the road to Bath, Maine, my foot suddenly lifts on the pedal, my hand turns the wheel and I head toward the small pulloff. I always stop to view it all, this landscape of my past, the broad spartina and salthay meadows. Whenever I do I am comforted to remember that along the Delaware, sunsets still come through the refracting mists, barn owls still prowl the meadows, and congregations of fireflies light the marshes in mysterious glowing orbs. I know it shall be so, long after I have disappeared, after the fiddlers have retreated to the cloistered shelter of the mudbanks, and after the last red berry has fallen on a remembered country road, deep in the snows of December.

Light breaks where no sun shines;
Where no sea runs, the waters of the heart
Push in their tides.

—Dylan Thomas

sunrise on the Sheepscot

Sunrise

The first rays of light began to tip over the edge of the horizon, a diffused shallow bowl of illumination, scumbling into the deep blue darkness still holding the planet Venus and a little slip of crescent moon. A cold front had passed in the night, and with it the September sea foamed in frothy white breakers that hissed along the shore. Out over the Atlantic a touch of palest pink crept along the distant cloud bank, then receded into deeper waters.

I stood at the top of the dune and watched as the glowing warmth lifted higher, brushing the base of the clouds in rose then grazing flecks of light along the ridge of cumulous.

I could hear her then, coming up behind me, feeling the mounded sand compressing under her steps as she labored to reach the summit of the dune. I did not look back. I knew she was wearing a blue kerchief on her head, and the navy blue sweater that hung by the door, and that she was thin, oppressively thin, with brown eyes becoming larger as the flesh of her face became taunt and nearly transparent. For months now, she had struggled, and we, her family, had struggled with her. My mother had acquired a kind of ethereal quality in the past weeks, as of a being that is not quite of this world, but on another plane, that otherland of the dying. I knew all of this and held out my hand, open, stretched away from my side, knowing she would take it when she reached me.

The sky above was expanding slowly, pushing the darkness farther overhead, touched oddly with that tint of green where it meets the blue. On the horizon the rose fractured into a prism of violets, with fingers of vermillion higher up and edging some curling cirrus clouds. She touched my hand then, holding it tightly. I knew, again without turning, that she was facing seaward, and that her eyes were full of the light, and that there were no words we needed. We had said them all, so many times over the past months, in the stillness of summer evenings on the wicker porch, or in hospital rooms, amid the cold indifference of the staff that hurried in and out, adjusting bed sheets, taking her pulse, looking at the swelling in the abdomen that signaled the advance of disease. So now we were quiet together, alone in the presence of the unfolding sunrise breaking open the world in the heart of September.

***

"Do you think I might be able to go to the shore again?" she had said in those waning days of August as she lay on the wicker settee, her eyes never looking at me, only staring unfocused in the distance. Beside her rested unread magazines and correspondence, cards from well-meaning friends, an African violet struggling to hold on to its remaining leaves. The house had a stale quality, neither dirty nor clean, but in a transition to a kind of spiritless sterility.

"Sure," I said confidently, knowing she could not do this on her own, and wondering if she was really up to such a venture. "What would you like to do?"

"I think I'd like to go back to Sea Isle for a few days. I'd like to wade in the ocean again. Do you think we could do that?" She was asking, but it was almost a plea, not to me, but rather like a question to herself.

I looked at her sallow face, the yellow tinge around the eyes, and saw her hand raise shakily and brush the hair from her forehead, the hand I had known all my life, the first

58

memory, the hand at the soft breast, the hand plucking blue-berries in summer, wiping floors, plaiting my hair, rolling piecrusts, the hand of hanging laundry and clean sheets, the mending hand of socks and spirits, prom dresses and band-aged knees, capable like a pilgrim, unadorned except for the gold wedding band and little diamond engagement ring, the hand whose veins I knew as closely as my own. And in that moment I would have slogged through the fires of Hell to give her this wish.

"Of course," I said. "I'll find us a place and we'll do it."

"Do you think I could go look too?" she asked.

The next day we left for the shore. I condensed the visits to realtors into short intervals because she was so very tired. After looking at two apartments she left the remainder of the inspections to me. I felt stressed and knew the task was wearing on her, so I chose a place impulsively, a not very glamorous downstairs apartment, but one in a house on a street just two blocks from the site of our old summer cot-tage. There were few residences nearby, and the house backed up to a dune where foxtail reeds and bayberry thrived amid the sea roses and wild morning glories. The sounds of the ocean flowed through open east windows that caught sea breezes in the afternoon. I returned to the realtor and left a deposit for the third week in September.

***

After Labor Day, summer crowds desert the beach, aban-doning the shore in one congested exodus, ignoring the finest month of the year and leaving the coast to sea gulls and sandpipers, and the few people able to manage a fall vaca-tion. We came then, when the days were still summer-like, but the evenings pleasantly cool with a hint of fall in the cloudless nights. I packed all the suitcases and enough food for the first few days. The kitchen and bath were not partic-ularly clean after a summer of rotating tenants, and I scoured fixtures, made beds, then heated a pot of vegetable soup for our first evening meal. Afterwards I moved our clothing into hanging closets, unpacked toiletries, and we settled in.

My father preferred to stay at home and would only visit occasionally. He was finding it difficult to deal with mother's illness and was, unknown to me, becoming profoundly depressed and sometimes confused. In some way, it seemed he viewed me as a nurse, a person impersonally charged with relieving him of something of a burden.

For my own husband, the demands of work meant that he was unable to join us as well, and so the experience became, for my mother and myself, an opportunity to spend uninterrupted time together.

Very quickly, in the manner that lost routines are resurrected after the passage of many years, we settled into the rhythm of an old forgotten beach life. We rose with the sun, beginning each day with a walk along the tideline, sometimes pausing to sit in the soft sand and watch the silken morning ocean breakers. After each walk, we accumulated a fresh store of sea glass, driftwood, and assorted shells. These we piled on the backstep, near the hose where we washed the sand from our feet.

Mother collected bouquets of bayberry and rose hips for the mayonnaise jar that sat in the sun on our kitchen table. Here she would instruct me over the bayberry leaves with her recipes for making clam chowder, or seasoning spaghetti sauce like Smitty and his wife used to do. It seemed to me that she somewhat compulsively planned these menus, devoting inordinate amounts of time to organizing the meals. But as she lost her appetite and could eat less, she became more fixated on "what might taste good". I always cooked what she wanted, and never chastised her for not eating more. This was beyond her control, the course of a disease which robbed her, day by day, of a once beautiful and capable body.

It was that frail and beloved body, enclosing her beautiful spirit, that stood with me on a dune in the September morning. Like two children we watched, forgetful of the sorrow, as the ambient light grew warmer, reflecting off the windows of the houses lining the beach. I could see that her face was mutely silhouetted beside me. And even though the sun had not appeared, its presence was all around, hinted in the streaming crests of breakers, in the cloud bank transforming into shades of soft purple, and fanning the upper air with rays that obliterated the last remnant of a dying moon. The sea was eerily quiet, the atmosphere tentative and weightless, as if the returning light were confirmed in the very molecules of air that waited motionlessly to receive it....

Then the first thin rim of sun broke above the sea. It strobed gold across the waves, painting the shadowed foam in deep cerulean blue and infusing the grasses and the dunes and the surrounding air with light. In a single transforming moment a day broke full and wide across the deep Atlantic.

She spoke then.

"I've never seen a sunrise as beautiful as this, Belva Ann."

I stood there, hardly able to catch my breath. Neither had I, and I do not know why this was so.

We stayed on a long time and watched as the waves flicked rosy sea smoke in their curls and the first gulls drifted in from the marshes to greet the sun.

***

For many hours that week, mother sat in a folding beach chair, placed at the edge of the water where she would write in her diary, her feet comforted by the waves. Sometimes she would hold the pen poised above the page, staring idly, writing nothing. At such times I sat quietly with her, doing little water color studies of waves, trying to cast from my mind anything but the reality of the moment. In the afternoons she usually slept on the sofa in the living room, getting strength for the evening and perhaps a visit from my father. We were in bed by 9 o'clock, then up again with the sunrise for coffee at the breakfast table.

Both of us, that week in September, had no patience for putting things off, for the limitations of time were never far from our minds. We did things spontaneously, without planning or structure. We went to the boardwalk and made gaudy necklaces from puka shells, bought huge boxes of Copper Kettle fudge or saltwater taffy, and purchased stacks of postcards we never intended to mail. And mostly we talked. We talked about my father and our concerns for his future, about mother's memories of our family, and about our love for each other...about how grateful we were to have been mother and daughter. Sometimes we talked about what might lie ahead.

"Do you think it will come easily?" she asked. The question came out of nowhere, insinuating itself between the gentle throbbing of the waves.

I sat beside her on the sand, doing a small watercolor, the pounding around us matching the sound of a human pulse.

"I don't want to linger when I can no longer be of any good to anyone. Tell me what the doctor says, because he won't talk to me."

I put my arm around her shoulders and was startled by the unfamiliar feel of bone. It was 70 degrees, but her skin felt cold. How can you tell your mother what she already knows, but doesn't know? What can you say when you love someone so much that you would gladly give your own life if it would ease her pain? I hesitated——looking at her eyes— they were questioning, and trusting me for truth.

"The doctor says he does not expect much pain," I began..."He says you will probably just get more tired...and go into a coma...That's probably how it will happen."

The waves continued their soft thrumming. She sighed,

"I'm so glad to know that. Thank you, honey."

Thank you? I suppressed an urge to run far into the dunes, to pull at the grass, to weep and flail till there was nothing left to feel. But instead I turned to my pointless watercolor and saw the colors blur into watery sameness. I held her then. There was nothing left to say. Untruths, I suppose, are luxuries of those with time. Comfort then was only found in honesty, and in the patient presence that is the last gift of loving. For that final gift, one which we gave each other, I will be forever grateful....and for that week at the coast, an imperishable memory to hold for the time ahead.

***

The first rays of pink light filter through my bedroom window. I pull on my old clothes and a warm breaker and walk out into the chill morning air. I am moving slower now; I walk with a cane and my knees are weak. I am no longer the young woman I once was, but I'm drawn still to the promise of a brilliant sunrise in the nascent wisps of color reaching into the eastern sky. I adjust my windbreaker and climb the long hill overlooking the Sheepscot River, then turn slowly to face the coast. The passage of thirty years has not dimmed her memory, nor have the experiences of a life diluted the singular vision of a moment. I remember all of this, and do not look back, but hold my hand open, stretched away from my side. And I wait.

Men go abroad to wonder at the heights of mountains, at the huge waves of the sea and the long courses of rivers, at the vast compass of the ocean, at the circular motions of the stars, and they pass by themselves without wondering.
—Saint Augustine

evening on the marsh

The Compass

It all comes around again. "Jack died three weeks ago," the letter began. "He thought a lot of you."

The letter was folded with other correspondence in a desk drawer. For six years I had not looked at it. Of course, I knew it was there, wrapped with a small bundle of letters I had retained with me when we moved north a few years ago. Today I read the words again, remembering the man I barely knew but who had walked into my life after an absence of fifty years to deliver a message from someone long dead.

What had motivated him to reach out after such a long silence remains a mystery to me, as much, I suspect, as it was to him. Perhaps in retrospect he sensed some end approaching and wanted to unburden himself of something he had been carrying for a long time. Now, as I looked at the letter, it seemed he was reaching out again.

"Jack went very peacefully," his wife wrote. In the restrained courtesy of one not wishing to expose friends to too much grief or death, she had kept her comments minimal.

I knew it was cancer that had claimed him finally. The same disease that had eventually taken my mother and my uncle Bob, silently eating away their flesh until they were both cadavers that somehow still breathed yet were hollowed out inside. I had stood by my mother's bedside and watched her die. And now Jack was gone too, receding into a collective memory where he was conjoined with my mother and uncle in a way more intimate than he knew in life. Yet I might never have known him at all except for his unusual appearance on a farm lane long ago, and I might never have resolved my decision to come north were it not for this solitary visit.

Sometimes it seems that there were other events, other faces that now fit into some larger pattern. I struggle to fit the pieces together, to make some sense of it. Yet Jack has died, and I will never know what led him to my house, what brought him down that lane at the precise moment when I was struggling with a question he could not know, nor even answer. Nor why it all comes back now as I try to fulfill my vow to write it down, a promise made when I put the letter away six years ago.

I remember the day he appeared, and the feeling of being torn from the umbilical cord of my former life, a displacement of a magnitude I could never have imagined. When you've lived in a place for so long, every tree and shoreline, house and field has a significance and is the repository of a memory. For a landscape painter, the loss is doubly intense because the essence of one's art is the touchstone of memory that fills a canvas more surely than the pigments or superficialities of subject matter. So the leaving became an enormous fracturing, both creatively and personally, and I was profoundly troubled.

I had slept poorly. My recurring bouts of Lyme Disease worsened. I questioned the direction I was heading. Yet if it was possible to lose direction and still function, I was doing that, for I worked in order to remediate the questions and the pain. Our house had become a labyrinth of boxes, a sorting station for piles to be discarded, piles to be given away, piles to be packed. But everything I touched contained an experience, and the internal boxes stacked in my head like the cardboard containers precariously balanced throughout the house.

It was into this chaotic clutter that an elderly, ruddy-faced man appeared one morning. He was carrying a box under his arm and I had the fleeting impression that he might be a salesman, although he looked too ill at ease. Maybe he was lost, like me.

I opened the door and probably raised my brows in a questioning look.

He paused briefly, studying my face.

"I bet you don't remember me," he said tentatively. His face was round and his eyes were the blue of a cerulean sea. I noticed his huge hands, the way he made them into fists, then relaxed them as though working out an arthritic stiffness. They were a workingman's hands, I reasoned, accustomed to some kind of hard physical labor.

I saw nothing familiar however and I guess my lack of a reaction generated the quick follow-up, "but I remember you."

"I'm sorry..." I started to apologize, but he hastily continued, upping the ante.

"And I remember you with your Grandfather Cap." He made a movement referencing my height I presumed, somewhere around knee level, and as he did so he blinked his eyes reflexively, a startled quality, several times, then waited.

From a doorway somewhere far back in a house no longer existing I saw a young man standing on a back porch, dressed in his military uniform. There was a kind of nervous tick in the blue eyes, something acquired in a place called Korea. One of his hands shook slightly as he turned his handsome face to me. I was very young but already captivated. Then my mother suddenly called, her voice rising from the backyard where she was hanging clothes, "Hi Jack! You're home!"

I strangely heard another voice now, my own, calling with her across a gulf of years. It was then that the face before me crinkled into a wide smile. Jack had come home again.

***

The afternoon that followed was full of Jack's stories about life on the bay and his experiences as a young boy. His father had worked for the railroad and was, it seemed, disinterested in him and seldom home. My grandfather, who had lived nearby, had taken Jack under his wing during his impressionable teen years, even giving him odd jobs on the *Warfield*. Jack had washed decks, hauled bushel baskets of oysters to the shuckers, and sometimes was allowed to steer the *Warfield* through the spindly stakes that marked the leased grounds of the watermen. Jack had obviously enjoyed the attention of my grandfather and felt that he had given him an important job as a full member of the crew.

"But you know, the best thing about those days and Cap's boat was them breakfasts—and he had a good cook in that galley. That was 1930, you know, and nobody had much money then, especially them that was crewin' and workin' the bay bottom. Cap's cook, well, he made these pancakes as thick as my thumb, and he buried 'em in butter." Jack licked a lower lip, "And those days you kept a crew if you had a good cook below."

His eyes looked away and I knew he was seeing it as it all had been, seeing the ship, smelling the aromas of the galley as if in a beloved dream of his boyhood. Then he shifted in his chair, still flexing the huge hands.

"You ever go out with Cap?" he asked, squinting his eyes.

"No," I confessed. "I was only on the boat one time I can remember. I was pretty young you know."

"Yea. I guess you wouldn't have known it, but there was so many things about your grandfather that I couldn't never figure. Those old watermen, they knew things that we never will. Like I could never figure how your grandfather could get right into the middle of his oyster grounds in a pea soup fog so thick that you couldn't barely see the front o' the boat. We'd go out into that bay and not a single marker would be in sight, but when the fog would lift we'd be right over Cap's plantin' grounds. Smack in the middle. And he didn't have no fancy equipment then, no landmarks of any kind to steer by. I used to think he could navigate by the smell of the water."

As Jack talked, I perceived there was some pain between his words, some wound he still carried, maybe many woundings, perhaps from his childhood, perhaps from the war. It is hard to know where a man's life has taken him, what troubles he has known, but it was apparent that something about my grandfather's attention had been important at a time when a young boy had little direction or guidance.

Such things were not directly discussed that day, for Jack was of a generation that did not dwell on self-reflection or analysis, but rather spoke through their stories. And so that afternoon we talked as people do who have a shared yet largely unknown past, who try to find the particular roads where their paths may have intersected, along with the people who were their companions from very different perspectives of age and time.

As the hours passed I recall I kept wondering about the package that was lying beside Jack's chair. I felt it was something for which our conversation was a kind of prelude.

After many cups of coffee Jack finally reached down and lifted the mysterious box with great care, almost reverence, placing it on the coffee table in front of me. I noticed that his eyes were glazed and sad.

"This is something Cap gave to me," he said, "and I think he'd want you to have it. I don't know why I didn't do this sooner, but I just felt I should do it now."

I stared at the object on the table...a dove-tailed wooden box. I opened it and saw a beautiful brass ship's compass inside.

"It's from the *Warfield*," Jack said simply.

I was momentarily uncomprehending. I couldn't believe that anything of the *Warfield* survived, much less that it should find its way to me after a passage of nearly half a century. Lifting the box and holding it on my lap, I looked at the needle of the compass—the ship's compass that had guided a man who worked his whole life on the Delaware Bay, that had steered a vessel in fog and storms and finally been given to a young man who had silently treasured it all his life. Now the needle wavered and settled quietly. It pointed North.

***

I carefully place the compass back on the desk and continue rummaging around in the little bundle of notes. Among them is the only letter I ever received from Jack, one written shortly after our move to Maine and several months before his death. In part it reads, "The lessons I learned from your Grandfather have directed me many times on the right path. I am more than satisfied that the compass has gone on a true course to where it belongs."

The compass has surely directed me, more than he could have known. The source is true. It points due North, straight over the roof of our barn and across the golden ridge of the Sheepscot hills. It insistently reminds me that home survives in the memories of the people and places I cherish.

The compass retains a prominent place on a secretary desk in the living room, next to an antique spyglass and some family photos. The room is part of a sea captain's house in a town that once built coastal schooners, a house that looks over a tidal river that flows out a long peninsula into the Gulf of Maine. When I look at the compass I am reminded of my past, reminded that for me there is only one point of reference. It is internal, molded in water and memory, carried as the tides that draw down and return each day.

I fold Jack's letter back into the little packet and return it to the desk drawer. "Thank you, Jack," I whisper. I have kept my promise. Somewhere in the house a door softly closes. It is growing late.

my parents and myself

our beach house

our cottage after the storm

me with a beach friend

three of my grandfather's ships
("Warfield" on left)

my mother and grandfather

Uncle Bob on an oyster boat

me with my beach friends

my grandfather on the "Warfield"

author and her husband Lew, 1985

Resources

The Delaware Estuary: Rediscovering a Forgotten Resource
edited by Tracey L. Bryant and Jonathan R. Penneck, 1988.

"Great New Jersey Coastal Storms of the 20th Century,"
Wet Water Video Company, 1995.

Lighthouse to Leeward Margaret Louise Mints, 1976.

Seasons of the Salt Marsh David Alan Gates,
Chathan Press, 1975.

Walking the Wetlands by Janet Lyons and Sandra Jordan,
John Wiley and Sons, Inc., 1989.

Natural Lives, Modern Times by Bruce Stutz,
Crown Publishers, Inc., 1992.

Salt Marsh Diary by Mark Seth Lender,
St. Martin's Press, 2011.

The End of Nature by Bill McKibben, Random House, 1989.

About the Author

Belva Ann Prycel is a native of Millville, New Jersey, who grew up near the Delaware bayshores and Atlantic coast of which she so often writes. A graduate of Rowan College, an artist and former teacher, her paintings have been exhibited in museums, colleges, and galleries throughout the U.S. In 2001, she was one of four artists profiled in a New Jersey Network Public Television presentation, "Bayshore Artists: Celebrating Our Sense of Place."

Prycel has illustrated two books and was a frequent cover artist for South Jersey Magazine. Her writing has appeared in regional magazines, environmental journals, and two national anthologies.

In 2002, she moved to Sheepscot Village, Maine, with her husband Lewis and their dogs, Jolie and Tucker. Since that time, Prycel has written and illustrated three books of non-fiction, *Times and Tides, Water Tales,* and *Passage*, all memoirs of the coast and of her family. She currently enjoys painting, writing, living near water, and playing ragtime piano.

She may be contacted at baprycel@roadrunner.com

www.ingramcontent.com/pod-product-compliance
Lightning Source LLC
Chambersburg PA
CBHW040929030426

42334CB00002B/16